Connecting Entrepreneurs, Philanthropists and Influencers.

BUSINESS
BOOSTER TODAY MAGAZINE
THE #1 GERMANY BASED MAGAZINE FOR THE GLOBAL ENTREPRENEUR

VOLVO XC40
100% ELECTRIC SUV

CONTENT

COVER STORY

The Volvo XC40 Recharge is innovative, smart and beautiful

A product introduction by
Christian Bartsch
Editor in Chief & Publisher

6

STARTUPS

Cashflow Guidance

Startups need the right guidance to generate cashflow in time.

Christian Bartsch

17

6	The Volvo XC40 Recharge is innovative, smart and beautiful Christian Bartsch	22	How to manage your business's global compliance risks, with lessons from Facebook John Bostwick
12	My Most Important Business Principles Brandon Steiner	25	English Access Guateng ... Interview with Founder Dean Graham
14	What a month without flying did for Me Raluca Gomeaja	27	Stockholm: The Unicorn Factory of The World Asa Granberg
15	Is digital marketing really the most essential part of any marketing strategy Tom Jungen	28	70 years of friendship between Germany and the USA Sue Baumgärtner-Bartsch
17	Start-Ups need the right Guidance to get Cashflow going Christian Bartsch	31	Using Geo-Fencing in online advertising Andrew Walker
18	The Hotel Munich Palace Sue Baumgärtner-Bartsch		
20	The Importance of Networking & Top Tips to be more effective. Part 1 of 3 – 'Do's' John Stokoe		

CONNECT WITH US

Read more Business Booster Today Magazine content at BusinessBoosterToday.com

Download the **Business Booster Today App** for iPhone or Android.

Like the **Business Booster Today Magazine on Facebook** for the latest news, photos, videos and exclusive online content.

Follow **@mybbtmagazine** on Twitter and keep informed on breaking news and business trends.

View stories and photos on Instagram and get a backstage insight. Follow us at **businessboostertoday**

Make connections with fellow entrepreneurs and business people in our community at businessboostertoday.com

FOUNDER'S CORNER

BY SUE BAUMGÄRTNER-BARTSCH

The fourth quarter of 2019 has been a very festive one, as our VP and lead editor has been invited to a **royal event** in Germany, which has been celebrating 70 years of friendship between America and Germany. See her article for a behind the scenes coverage. But not only do we care about Germany and the USA. We value building business relationships that span the globe. As we meet and interview people from around the world, whether these are start-ups, innovators or people with a keen eye for the good in society and beyond the border, we enjoy to bring you a variety of entrepreneurs and entrepreneurial thinking brands and companies to your attention.

Being connected with industry leaders and hearing their input and feedback is what consistently prompts us to change and to improve. Niche areas, such as "FinTech", for example, are playing a bigger role now and as we move into the 1st and 2nd quarter of 2020.

The **Swedish Start Up and Tech environment** is currently **boiling hot** and the **Swedish Unicorns** are hitting the world and the **stock exchanges** like never before. You do not want to miss out as we cover more on these markets and industries. In this edition, we share with you why Stockholm is considered to rival Silicon Valley as the tech unicorn factory of the world.

The Business Booster Today magazine travelled last month to **Berlin Germany** to meet up with the head of marketing of an **international entertainment** company. And even in Germany, we could not escape the Swedish brands. Are **Scandinavian brands** dominating? In the 14 days of travelling through Germany, we have seen so many amazing brands from Sweden, Denmark and Norway, such as the "Happy socks" in Munich Airport and then "Marabou" chocolate in a shop in Berlin, just to name a few.

As we are obsessed with **our vision to empower 20 million people** to take their business to the next level, we have not stopped to grow the global impact of our joint activities. Therefore, we have achieved to position the magazine in leading 5-and 6-star hotel chains worldwide. As you unwind from your flight, you can now enjoy our magazine in a comfortable setting in your hotel room with a cup of tea or coffee. Hotel chains that provide that feeling of restfulness, unwinding opportunity with a cutting edge, such as the "The Flemings Group", The "Hotel Palace Munich", "Kempinksi" hotels, and "Mandarin Oriental", are already offering our magazine.

In fact, we met up with the management of one of the most luxurious hotels in Munich Germany, the "Hotel Palace Munich", which is part by the Kuffler Group to see their wonderful extension of their hotel rooms, the winter garden, and got a special VIP tour of the hotel. It was fascinating to see how much the management team cares for their guests and clients, and how the hotel constantly strives to not stand still but to move with the time, how they think innovatively and is open for new input.

Business is all about building relationships, and we value quality over quantity, follow ups and follow throughs.As Business Booster Today magazine is now flying around the world, reaching millions of people, how are you leading your business and life? We met so many people and they fly from one place to the next, and when we asked them whether they enjoy flying constantly, the answer is still a big YES.

Why is this? Flying provides the entrepreneur with **freedom, speed and clarity**.

Entrepreneurs, innovators, thought leaders have all one thing in coming: They **embrace the change**, and keep an eye on what **is coming** next. Change is something that keeps successful entrepreneurs and leaders excited and is not something to be resisted. And that readiness for change only comes with a bigger purpose, a clarity that you gain when you look over the clouds and step outside the boundaries.

As we mark **30 years of reunification** of Germany, we look back on the one hand to see what has once divided as a nation. Simultaneously, we look at the presence and the future, which shows that friendship, fruitful business relationships, thinking ahead for generations to come and connecting and uniting is at the core. The ability to **connect with people** is what drives CEOs to create and expand their companies to a higher level. The conscious entrepreneur is in the making. And this requires to be able to interact and do business with **empathy and authenticity**. Profitability is no longer the key driver what sets businesses apart. Success is gaining a new meaning as people strive to challenge companies to provide products and services that are not only innovative and disrupting, but also in line with the good for society, **raising the consciousness** of leaders and influencers on a massive scale.

Business Boosters are **change makers, disruptors and entrepreneurs** with a vision. We give a voice to people, products and brands. We not only build brands; we make them known! With the edition of the Business Booster Today Magazine and our upcoming special editions, we are showcasing conscious-driven entrepreneurs, leading CEOs, thinktanks and influencers and are providing a platform to share knowledge, to build bridges and to feature the **movers and shakers of the business world.**

EDITORIAL TEAM

Christian Bartsch
Publisher & Editor in Chief

John Stokoe
Property Editor

Jim Paar
Editor

Udo Bartsch
Business Editor

Melody Garcia
Social Conscious Leadership Editor

Eren Ünlü
Technology Editor

Sue Baumgärtner-Bartsch
VP & Interview Editor

Douglas Vermeeren
Leadership Editor

Stefanos Sifandos
Editor

Jan Erik Horgen
Investment Editor

Greg JC Granier
Entertainment Industry Editor

Michael Knulst
Business Editor

IMPRESS

ISSN (Print Edition)
2627-9223

ISSN (Online Edition)
2627-9231

PUBLICATION DATE
24.11.2019

PUBLICATION SERIES INFO
November 2019 No. 9

PUBLICATION REVISION ID
2019-11-24--1

PUBLISHER & EDITOR IN CHIEF
Christian Bartsch

LEAD EDITOR & VP
Sue Baumgaertner-Bartsch

CONTRIBUTING EDITORS
Udo Bartsch, Douglas Vermeeren, Melody Garcia, Jan Erik Horgen, Michael Knulst, Louis Kotze, Marina Kotze, John Stokoe, Eren Ünlü, Greg JC Granier

CONTRIBUTING WRITERS
John Bostwick, Michelle Davis, Robb Evans, Raluca Gomeaja, Sam Komeha, Katrin Israel, Jaine Lopez, Tom Jungen, Danijela Nakovski, Milos Nakovski, Jim Paar, Nina Peutherer, Richard Peutherer, Nina Schmid, Kirstie Shapiro, Stefanos Sifandos, Cristina Stavinski, Brandon Steiner, Mona Tenjo, Yasemin Yazan, Erwin Wils, Sabine Zettl

PHOTOGRAPHY
Editors & Advertisers

VIP STYLING & MAKEUP
Aldrin-David Verburgt

PUBLISHED BY
ACATO GmbH, 1st. Floor, Theresienhoehe 28, 80339 Munich, Germany

ADVERTISING & SALES
sales@businessboostertoday.com

Phone +49 89 54041070

www.businessboostertoday.com

SUBSCRIPTIONS

Booster club members: annual membership dues include €197 for a regular one-year subscription and €47 for an electronic member subscription. Non-members subscription rate are €97 for an electronic subscription. Change of address notices and subscriptions should be directed to BBT magazine.

Although BBT Magazine maybe quoted with proper attribution, no portion of this publication may be reproduced unless written permission has been obtained from the publisher.
The views expressed in this magazine are those of the authors and might not reflect the official policies of Publisher and its associated organisations.

The editors assume no responsibility for unsolicited manuscripts but will consider all submissions. Contributors' guidelines are available at businessboostertoday.com. Business Booster Today Magazine is a double-blind, peer-reviewed publication.

To order reprints, visit businessboostertoday.com or email info@businessboostertoday.com.

©2018 ACATO GmbH. "Business Booster Today", "Business Booster Today Magazine", "Booster Club", "Booster TV", "Crypto Booster Magazine", "BBT", the Magazine logo and related trademarks, names and logos are the property of ACATO GmbH, and are registered and/or used in Germany, the European Union and countries around the world.

All Content is protected intellectual property and may not reproduced without written consent of the publisher.

THE VOLVO XC40 IS INNOVATIVE, SMART AND BEAUTIFUL.

A product introduction by the Publisher

BY CHRISTIAN BARTSCH (GERMANY)

Volvo aims to maximise **zero-tailpipe- emission** electric driving by reimbursing motorists for their energy costs and encouraging them to keep their car's hybrid battery charged.

Volvo is committed to **driving down carbon emissions** with the recently declared ambition to become a global carbon-neutral business by 2040. Just how much energy each customer uses will be monitored via the **Volvo On Call app**.

This logs how much power the car consumes, and also allows the owner to monitor the charge status of their car's battery via their mobile device.

Market-leading plug-in hybrid range

Volvo leads the European market in offering a plug-in hybrid version of every model in its range, so whether buyers are seeking a saloon, estate car or SUV, the **stylish Swedish brand** has every base covered. The recently launched XC40 T5 plug-in hybrid premium compact SUV is ahead of the European automotive market. With a 180hp petrol engine and an 82hp electric motor, it is the most efficient version of the multi-award-winning XC40, offering official fuel economy of up to 141.1mpg (WLTP Combined cycle) and CO_2 emissions from just 38g/km.

Volvo's carbon-neutral ambition

The free electricity initiative is just one element in Volvo's far-reaching plans to achieve a substantial reduction in the lifecycle carbon footprint of all its new cars.

The company recently announced its intention to achieve a cut of 40% between 2018 and 2025, a key step towards its goal of **becoming a climate-neutral business by 2040**.

By adopting cleaner, electrified powertrains, it will bring down overall tailpipe emissions by 50% by 2025, while also working to significantly **reduce the environmental impact of its manufacturing**, supply chain, logistics and other operations,

targeting a 25% reduction by 2025.

From next year, the first question asked of visitors to Volvo's customer website will be whether they want their car with a plug, or not.

At the same time, a **new Recharge branding** will be introduced for the company's growing range of plug-in hybrid and fully electric cars.

If that was not enough innovation for you, then you need to look at what Volvo is doing in regards to combining digital technology and environmental consciousness.

Volvo implements blockchain traceability of cobalt used in electric car batteries

Volvo Cars will become the first car maker to implement global traceability of cobalt used in its batteries by applying blockchain technology. The announcement follows the reveal last month of the company's first fully electric car, the XC40 Recharge.

What is cobalt? Cobalt is a chemical element found in the Earth's crust only in chemically combined form, save for small deposits found in alloys of natural meteoric iron.

Cobalt-based blue pigments (cobalt blue) have been used since ancient times for jewelry and paints, and to impart a distinctive blue tint to glass, but the color was later thought to be due to the known metal bismuth. Currently it is mostly mined in Canada and the Kongo region.

The **traceability of raw materials** used in the production of lithium-ion batteries is one of the main sustainability challenges faced by car makers.

Volvo Cars is committed to full traceability. Thereby Volvo is ensuring that customers can drive electrified Volvos knowing the **material** for the batteries has been **sourced responsibly**.

Blockchain technology significantly boosts transparency of the raw material supply chain because the

information about the material's origin cannot be changed undetected. Blockchain establishes a transparent and reliable shared data network. The data in the blockchain includes the cobalt's origin, attributes such as weight and size, the chain of custody and information establishing that participant's behavior is consistent with OECD supply chain guidelines.

This approach helps create trust between participants along a supply chain.

You will be wondering where trend is going and who the hidden champions are. For many car manufacturers who have a century of experience in manufacturing combustion based cars, it is not easy to maintain its USP while dealing with a totally disruptive concept.

XC40 Recharge is Volvo's first ever fully electric car

Volvo Cars introduces the XC40 Recharge, the company's first ever fully electric car and the first model to appear in its brand-new Recharge car line concept.

The XC40 Recharge is based on the **multi-award-winning and best-selling XC40 small SUV**. It is the first of a family of fully

BUSINESS BOOSTER TODAY MAGAZINE 7

electric Volvos.

It represents a true milestone for the swedish car manufacturer. The company's first electric car and the first Volvo with a **brand-new infotainment system** powered by Google's Android operating system.

Recharge will be the **overarching name for all chargeable Volvos** with a fully electric and plug-in hybrid powertrain.

To further encourage electric driving, every Volvo Recharge plug-in hybrid model will come with **free electricity for a year**, provided through a refund for the average electricity cost during that period.

The XC40 Recharge is everything customers expect from a Volvo. With the addition of a fully electric all-wheel-drive powertrain the XC40 Recharge offers a **range of more than 400km (249 miles)** on a single charge and output of 408hp.

If you think you are a sitting duck when you buy into electtric cars then you need to rethink.

The battery charges to 80 per cent of its capacity **in 40 minutes** on a fast-charger system, which does not hold you up on long trips. That is enough time for a latte, a classic Swedish Princess Cake (*Klassisk prinsesstårta*) and moving your legs.

The Android-powered infotainment system is fully integrated with Volvo On Call, the company's digital connected services platform. Via Volvo On Call, plug-in hybrid drivers can track how much time they spend driving on electric power.

No more sticky notes with dates and fuel consumption trying to make sense of you cars true operational cost. Volvo has opened the doors to a new generation of cars that live on the authentic image of Swedish style and robust product designs.

Entertainment vs Infotainment

Volvo Cars is fundamentally rethinking infotainment in the forthcoming fully electric Volvo XC40. Powered by Android, the new infotainment system offers customers **unprecedented personalisation**. That comes with improved levels of intuitiveness and new embedded Google technology and services.

The new system offers full integration of Android Automotive OS. Thereby car owners benefit from with **real-time updates to services such as Google Maps, Google Assistant and automotive apps** created by the global developer community.

The electric XC40 is also the first Volvo that will receive software and operating system updates over the air.

The fully electric XC40 is the first car to receive larger over-the-air updates to its software and operating system. This places Volvo Cars at the forefront of automotive connected services.

This same rich and fresh map data will be used to improve the capabilities of the XC40's Advanced Driver Assistance Systems (ADAS) by providing important information such as speed limits and curves in the road to the car.

The new infotainment system will be fully integrated with Volvo On Call, offering very convenient new features.

No more unpleasant surprises in

the morning. The **monitoring of battery status** and charging levels helps you avoid breakdowns.

For car owners of other brands you might be familiar with the **available upgrades like preheating**.

Volvo increases the convenience of technical features by combining intelligent technology and connectivity. Like to get your car on a cold winter's day pre-heated? Lost your car in the car park? Use the app to **find your car** in a large car park. Yes, other brands have similar features like remote locking and unlocking.

Vovlo has gone on step further to a **mobility solution**. How about car sharing via a digital key?

Sitting in cars can have an impact on the economy

Exclusive research by Volvo Car UK found more than a third of drivers have taken at least a day off work in the past year for back pain caused by poor-quality seats.

One in 10 drivers have had to ask for a full working week off for back pain from uncomfortable car seats. The pain is bad enough for nearly a third of drivers to see a doctor or physiotherapist. Volvo has been incorporating spinal research into its seat design since 1965, and specifically **uses softer materials and spring settings** for improved comfort and support.

Today, Volvo has a three-tier approach to seat comfort, focusing on **Initial Comfort, Cruising Comfort and Dynamic Comfort** – to ensure drivers and passengers remain relaxed and fully supported throughout their journey, regardless of the length or type of road.

More than one in 10 drivers also admitted (in the study) they had passengers refuse to get in their car because their seats were so uncomfortable.

Swedish design as we love it

"The roots of Scandinavian design are based on visual clarity and the reduction of element. The XC40 is a great example of this," said Robin Page, Head of Design at Volvo Cars. *"Its bold, instantly recognisable design is now even sleeker and more modern in the all-electric version. Without the need for a grille we have created an **even cleaner and more modern face**, while the lack of tailpipes does the same at the rear. This is the approach we*

will explore more and more as we continue down the road of electrification."

A covered front grille in body colour **creates a distinct visual identity** at the front of the car. This is made possible by the fact that an electric car needs less air flow for cooling purposes. The grille also neatly packages the many sensors. Eight exterior colours allow drivers to personalise their electric XC40. This includes a **brand new Sage Green metallic option**. A contrasting black roof comes as standard.

Two new 19" and 20" wheel options provide further opportunity for personalisation.

Inside, a brand new driver interface specifically designed for electric cars **keeps drivers up to date on relevant information** such as battery status, while the interior design package features sporty styling details as well as carpets made of recycled materials.

The battery pack is integrated into the floor of the car **without affecting interior space**. Volvo's Compact Modular Architecture (CMA) empowered designer to create a vehicle layout that has electrification in mind.

The wealth of **suitable and functional storage space** around the cabin remains in place. This is one of the major attractions for car owners of the XC40.

An **ingenious and radical new approach** to interior design provides XC40 drivers with more functional storage space in the doors and under the seats. Due to the spacial advantages of electric cars Volvo added a fold-out hook for small bags and a removable waste bin in the tunnel console.

The special front load compartment of the electric XC40 is located under the front bonnet. It provides around 30 litres of extra load space.

The author's conclusion

With the introduction of the "XC40 Recharge" Volvo Cars have jumped ahead of the race.

The XC40 an extremely innovative product of its kind. Furthermore, this is a beautiful car you can be proud to have parked in front of your house.

MY TWO MOST IMPORTANT BUSINESS PRINCIPLES:

BY BRANDON STEINER

BUSINESS ADVICE FROM SPORTS MARKETING GURU AND FORMER STEINER SPORTS FOUNDER & CEO BRANDON STEINER

When I coached my son Crosby's little league teams, I observed a vast array of motivational tactics on the part of the other coaches. For instance, when a team was winning but their players were losing focus, the coach would implore them to imagine they were getting pummeled.

"Play like we're 10 runs down!" he'd shout.

Likewise, when a team has virtually no chance of winning, it becomes a great indicator of who the best players are. Who's still launching himself out of the batter's box, scrapping his way to first? Who's still diving for balls? Who's still getting dirty?

Those are the **committed players**, who realize that **consistency over time** equals **credibility**. The ones who know that to be successful, you have to give your all, whether you're winning or losing. The most successful athletes I know say, "play the game, not the score."

Long time Steiner Sports client Mariano Rivera is a perfect example. The New York Yankee legend played hard during every inning, day in and day out, over the entire season. You can never tell what the score is from Mariano's body language during a given game. Even in the last game of the season, you wouldn't know if the Yankees were headed to the playoffs or if they were in last place in the American League East. For Mariano, every game, every inning, every pitch was game 7 of the World Series, bases loaded, two out, and a full count – there was no such thing as a "big game" or "big spot".

Entrepreneurs, employees -- everyone -- should perform the same way.

When you walk into your office, can you tell whether it's nine in the morning or six at night? Is it the beginning of a promising quarter -- or is it the end of a bad month? Are employees' stock options riding a promising wave, or slogging through a trough? None of these factors should matter. A valuable employee will look like a valuable employee no matter the situation and circumstances. Again, consistency over time equals credibility.

Too many salespeople misunderstand the unique importance of consistency. They have a big sales day, and to celebrate, they buy themselves a big lunch. Then, they leave work early because they feel they've earned it.

The days when you have a big sale -- when you're riding a big wave -- are the ideal days to go for a second big sale, a third, a fourth, and so on. In my experience, the best time to make more money is when you're already in the process of making money.

It's like Mariano Rivera on a save streak. If he had 5 straight saves, he would never go to his coach and say, "Skip, I have been doing pretty well this past week. I don't want to pitch today, I am good." The greatest competitors such as Mariano don't take days off, especially when they are hot, they want to ride the wave as long as they can.

In the hungry days at Steiner Sports, our office was only two blocks from Madison Square Garden. My connections afforded me a lot of Knicks and Rangers tickets; many nights after work I'd go to a game. And on most of those nights, I couldn't go home after the final buzzer. I'd go from the Garden right back to the office. My company was booming and I did whatever I could to ensure it continued on its upward trajectory.

Would you wake up every day at 5 a.m.? Would you regularly return to the office after an event at 11 p.m. on a weeknight? You might think you're giving 99 percent of yourself to something, but being all in means giving 100 percent. Either you're all in, or you're not.

As I tell my kids, the difference between 99% and 100% is not 1% - it's one hundred percent.

Playing the score and not the game is also unwise on an intrapersonal level. Do as much as you can, for as many people as you can, as often as you can, without expecting anything in return.

> "Don't worry about what you're getting back. Don't worry about how many dollars that person is going to equal for you. Being generous without keeping score strengthens your spirit, keeps you focused on the people who make your business what it is, and helps breed success."

I've always operated under this principle with the media. Back in the 1990s, when I was starting Steiner, the sports marketing industry was in its infancy. Even the journalists who were covering it didn't know too much about it. Whenever a reporter called me for a quote, guidance on a story, or to connect with the right person, I went out of my way to help not thinking or expecting they would help me or my company.

I built a reputation as the guy who could get players on the phone with journalists -- which made their lives a heck of a lot easier. I'd do whatever I could to help. I knew I wasn't getting much if anything back, but what I didn't realize was that unintentionally I was building greater credibility with the media, players, teams, and leagues.

I became such a trusted source that my name, and in turn, my company and brand, ended up in the media quite often. In the first 16 years of Steiner Sports, I didn't spend more than a hundred grand on advertising, promotion, and PR combined.

When you play the game, and not the score, you usually end up scoring more as a result and will probably gain more enjoyment by doing so.

Today, after thirty years of running Steiner Sports Marketing, I am onto my next chapter looking to **build upon the sports marketing and collectibles industries** I helped shape in the late eighties and early nineties. While the game has certainly changed, the business principles that made me successful have not – come with **intensity & passion** and **provide value to others** without expecting anything in return.

These two principles are the pillars of my new company The Steiner Agency, a group that helps businesses ranging from "mom & pop" shops to fortune 100 companies grow utilizing athlete talent. To be frank, I don't think my new company will be a success. I KNOW it will be given the group we have assembled and the mindset we have developed that is rooted in my most principles.

We are the little league team up 10-0, but still running out every ground ball, still diving, and always aware that our positive attitude will come back two-fold.

Wherever you are as a company or in your career, keep these principles in mind ✈

BUSINESS BOOSTER TODAY MAGAZINE 13

WHAT A MONTH WITHOUT FLYING DID TO ME

BY RALUCA GOMEAJA (FRANCE)

Travelling is one of my passions, and maybe one of yours. I grew up dreaming of travelling the world, I started to count the number of countries I've visited. Every time I am in a country I am proud and happy to learn a few words in the local language as sign of respect for people that I meet. From my corporate days I learned how to be in a country with people who work and live there instead of just being another tourist. I love people, I love the world and travelling was for me one of the best schools I ever attended.

Nowadays, between my personal life and my business I take a flight at least 1/week to keep it simple. And every so often I get asked the same question: why are you flying so much? Aren't you tired? My answer is mostly the same: this is what I love, and this is my choice. The only difference (which makes me quite sad) is that I imposed myself this rule: "no client no travel" (except for family members). Which means I don't get to see very important friends all over the world other than when my business brings me there. Lucky for me, I'm based in Paris and as the saying goes, "everyone loves Paris".

And yet, at one point in time, even my coach asked me "almost" the same question: what is that you are looking for? Meaning what is the real reason you travel so many days a year? You know how it goes, tons of people may ask exactly the same question, and one day, one person, may say it in a way that clicks. And despite the fact that I gave him the same answer, which is my deepest truth, I made a bet with myself, that I will purposely don't travel for a month. See what happens.

To be completely honest I did not plan for "when" that month to be, nor in which country, I just set this target in my head, so I get ready. It is also fair to say that it would have had probably a different result providing I would have chosen to be in a different environment for this month, or in a different setting; yet in the end, it was all up to me. So here I am, I took a month off from flying, almost from social media as well, and here are my results:

- I am more rested, which came as no surprise. Travelling is tiring even for people who love it.
- I am darker, and more fit, which considering my heaven location and my love for windsurfing is far from being a surprise as well. Yet all in all is so good to be back in shape and reconnect with my body.
- I am clearer. Which is one of the major benefits. Not only I did not travel but I did one month meditation challenge, which had a magic effect, every single day a new technique, and every single day something got clearer.
- I no longer ask myself the question which I hear so many times as well from others: are you happy? Like always we don't ask things that are obvious.
- I am calmer, in itself it is for me the highest transformation.
- My business benefits from it almost without me paying the effort, in that state of calm and rest, my mind got so much more business ideas and clarity, and new clients appeared "out of the blue".

We can all have different things that are addictive to us, in a way or another, or simply too much part of our life. We can even think this is our choice. Yet in the end, without taking the challenge for at least 28 days to see the effect, we may not know what we are missing. The main result for me is that travelling is a choice, I can still live and enjoy myself without it, yet there is a beauty in it that is definitely one of my life pleasures. The main change that came out of this experience is that I will allow myself these no flying breaks more often. What challenge are you ready to take for the next 28 days? Looking forward to read your experiences and learnings.

IS DIGITAL MARKETING REALLY
"THE MOST ESSENTIAL PART OF ANY MARKETING STRATEGY WHEN STARTING YOUR BUSINESS?"

BY TOM JUNGEN (CANADA)

Or...is Digital Marketing the one tool in your arsenal that you should skip when first starting your business? I reflect when I first had to decide where and how to start marketing my services. The overwhelmed feeling kicked in big time! The funny thing is that almost everyone will agree that marketing is essential; however, how to do that gets a lot more complicated. Of course, everyone has an opinion on what matters and how to do it. So, over the years, this is what I hear most often from small to **mid-sized businesses**:

• Oh, marketing it's too expensive; we do word of mouth (WOM). It's the best way.
• No need to market; if your product or service is excellent, people will find you no matter where you are.
• Printing brochures is very costly once you add graphics and printing plates.
• Newspaper, no one reads them anymore.
• Radio can't afford it.
• TV out of reach for small business owners.
• Google AdWords is too expensive, and people don't convert or buy.
• My all-time favourite is the following; "Facebook and Google AdWords doesn't work; it's all hype."

Now let me be blunt, as time is money. Let's have a look at each one, and I will give you my two cents worth: Is marketing expensive when starting your business? Hell yes! However, you can't afford not to invest in your business. Word of mouth (WOM), of course, you should talk it up and create hype. However, WOM will only get you so far and is what I consider a booster. What I would recommend is having WOM as an additive, just like salt and pepper, to augment the overall marketing strategy. As a stand-alone, you will be a dead man walking.

No need to market that's a non-starter. Printing brochures is one of the most expensive print versions available. My recommendation is that if you are starting out and working with a limited marketing budget, this one is on hold.

Newspapers? No one reads them anymore. Well, that makes me feel old. However, I agree that newspaper publications are not what they used to be since all things have gone online. However, I do have a heart for newspapers; seeing many proper placed ads for local markets can be very useful when strategically timed and placed. Radio? Can't afford it? You may be surprised as to the cost for 10 second and 30-second spot buys for your local businesses. This one surprises many business owners as they are pleasantly surprised by how competitive the rates have become in 2019. I encourage everyone to add this to your assortment of marketing tools.

Television is out of reach for small business owners. Yes, 100% agreed. I recommend this is where you make use of your smartphone. Take video clips to grab your potential clients' **attention** on Facebook, Instagram and YouTube. Just a note of caution here, your videos don't need to be professionally done. Save your money and keep pumping out essential videos with a **proper strategy** and messaging. I am rooting for you here till the cows come home! Next, we have Google AdWords: Too expensive. Sure, it costs money. Many individuals compare Facebook costs to Google AdWord costs. Don't mix up the two; they are entirely different machines. In many ways, Google AdWords is much more straightforward than Facebook. Why do you ask? The reason for this is that people searching on Google are already showing intent. These people are **actively searching** for a solution to their problem. This is key, as we now have an idea of the conversation going on in the online searchers' head. In short, these people are further along in the buying journey as they have already shown interest.

Just take a time out and think about this. What is the last thing you Googled? You are looking for something of interest or a solution to a problem. Facebook is very different because of it is known as **interruption marketing**. Meaning that people are not on Facebook actively seeking a solution for a problem. The chances are that they are looking for the exact opposite. They are looking for gossip, an escape from the office, and to catch up with family, friends and watch funny videos to chill. Herein lies the magic and **power of online digital marketing**, i.e., Facebook. You may have heard that Facebook collects an obscene amount of data. Let me repeat this...Facebook collects an obscene amount of data on its users, including where, what they visit and click on. Just to make sure I really get this point across well, read the following statement, not my opinion.

> "MIT Technology Review states that Facebook data is the most extensive data set ever assembled on human social behavior."

So, what does that mean? That means they know us better than we know ourselves. In number talk, that means Facebook has something like 400,000 data points on each of us. Yes, Facebook knows every single click we have made and trust me over time that paints a pretty good picture of each of us and what makes us tick and click. This is math on a large scale or what some call **AI machine learning**. Yes, it's powerful. This is exciting stuff. Are you with me? This means you can **target people** on Facebook with specific job titles, locations, schools, organizations, and so much more. Therefore, you can get very specific on each of your Ad campaigns, not just "Vanilla " blasting into a black abyss.

As you can see, this is why Digital Marketing really is "The Most Essential part of any marketing strategy when starting your business!" In summary, your marketing dollars can go much further on Facebook than anywhere else when done correctly. Maximize your marketing dollars, and achieve a low-cost and high impact with a Digital Marketing Strategy today.

START-UPS NEED THE RIGHT GUIDANCE TO GET CASHFLOW COMING IN

BY CHRISTIAN BARTSCH (GERMANY)

Many new companies in the technology field suffer from a massive cashflow issue as they focus far too long on building a perfect product or service. During this time more agile competitors will overtake them and drive them out of business.

In order to avoid running out of funds, these tech startups need a business coaching that is not based on standard recipies. Having founded several businesses and experienced the value of the business coach that helped me take my business to the next level, i do recommend to use of that.

Is it enough to have a coach?

No, you need to have a mentor that is willing to share with you his or her business experience. This will usually be an entrepreneur with more than 20 years business experience. In some cases you will find a former CEO for a subsidiary or major corporation that did not own the business but restructured the business.

Founders of technology companies are great analytic people. They can program software, develop hardware or come up with the most innovative chemical formula that replaces outdated manufacturing methods.

Schools and universities do not provides us with the necessary sales and new business development skills. These skills need to be learned outside of the outdated education system. Learning how to close a deal or how to create the first pitch of a product to the first corporate beta client .. that needs guidance.

Other skills you will develop as you go. Each time you have a client on the phone, you will learn my doing. It will be painful to be rejected but eventually you will know your pitch so well, that you do not think about it. It automatically comes with its customized structure out of you in response to the individual client's comments.

Having coached several business owners in Germany, UK, USA and Canada, I noticed that there was a lack of clarity how to get to a positive cash flow. Then i remembered having several check lists for our shipping, travels and flights.

That is why I then decided to reduce the complexity and to create easy to follow cheat sheets. That would make it easier for my clients to stay on track in between the coaching sessions we have. If you are interested, send me an email at info@gainyoursucess.com

THE HOTEL MUNICH PALACE

BY SUE BAUMGÄRTNER-BARTSCH

The Hotel Munich Palace: Drive for innovation, inspiration and attention to detail leaves every guest and business traveler with the highest satisfaction and appreciation

Early November 2019, the founders of the Business Booster Today magazine got a special behind the scenes VIP tour of the famous and exquisite Hotel Munich Palace- the Luxury 5 Star Boutique Hotel in the heart of Munich Germany. The Hotel Munich Palace is a personalized and family managed hotel and member of Preferred hotels and Resorts LVX. The hotel is part of the Kuffler group, which is one of the largest privately-owned food service companies in Germany.

We were inspired by the rooms and suites and their individual décor and focus on details. **16 new luxury rooms and suites** have been added in the spring of 2018 in the adjacent building. The new rooms all have marble baths and wooden floors and different elegant patterns and fabrics have been used to make these rooms stand out. Silk curtains and extraordinary parquet flooring highlights this ambience.

The newly added rooms and suites as well as the corridors invite guests with black and white photographs of Munich. We found out that **Stephan Kuffler**, the owner of the Kuffler group is not only an entrepreneur but also a fantastic photographer. His talent and contribution to this hotel and Munich is shared in his beautifully book, which is available on each desk in the new luxury rooms. For his hotel, he has chosen a special selection of different themes, such as the mountains, Munich, England and others, which brings in an urban and at the same time international atmosphere of the hotel.

One of the highlights of our tour was the **Presidential suite**, which has an open fire place, a private sauna with a private roof top garden and a view to the Church of Our Lady of Munich. There is luxurious space of the bedroom area with a walk-in-closet for the lady and one for the men. A heaven on earth for every woman. A Steinway piano is giving the suite an extra edge, and the Antiques from Asia and Africa give this suite an extra touch.

The spa and wellness area are small but exquisite and invites every business traveler for a successful and vital start into the day with day light and state of the art Techno gym equipment, right next to the roof terrace.

It was wonderful to hear that the **entertainment system** with the digital downloadable magazines in each room in different languages and niches also includes the **Business Booster Today** magazine; guests greatly enjoy to **read our magazine** and this gives the business guests and traveler the

additional value and service of a business magazine that is featuring the movers and shakers, the entrepreneurs, influencers and innovators and the other unique insights of the global business world.

The hotel has two elegant function rooms with day light. They have modern technical equipment for up to 36 persons and are the perfect places for executive meetings and special events. The rooms are light and elegant in design and have access to the rooftop terrace.

World class musicians, international business travelers and sophisticated tourists alike, enjoy the style, elegance and service provided by the hotel Munich Palace. Our VIP tour ended with a relaxing business lunch in the restaurant in the winter garden, which is the perfect oasis from the hustle and bustle of the city. We look forward to coming back in order to enjoy the afternoon tea before Christmas and many more occasions with our international guests and business partners to share more insights about the hotel and its future developments. ✈

THE IMPORTANCE OF NETWORKING & TOP TIPS TO BE MORE EFFECTIVE. PART 1 OF 3 – 'DO'S'

BY JOHN STOKOE (UNITED KINGDON)

Going to a networking event 'should' be about enhancing you or your business effectiveness. There are many reasons to attend the various events around, but simply put, one will learn from the successes and failures of attendees/speakers and ideally shortcut building key relationships needed in your business with like-minded and hopefully trusted colleagues. It stands to reason then, that honing your networking skills will make you more efficient with your time and maximise your 'return' on time spent at these events.

As a previous owner of an International Mastermind Network, I have made a note of my own and others behaviours, to create a guide designed to help attendees maximise their skills in the networking environment. Just turning up isn't enough, you need to be engaged and focussed. This is a three part guide dealing with Do's, Don'ts and Conversation starters.

Remember that One person, One Deal or One Opportunity can change your life or business forever.

This week is all about the Dos'

1. Do arrive prepared.

Know what you are looking for before you arrive, then you can build a strategy to ensure you achieve your purpose. What is the purpose of you being there? What are you trying to accomplish? If you are focussed on your desired outcome, you will get to that point quicker and spend less time on low priority tasks. You may be looking for a person or strong referral for a specific trade or skillset like a plumber (can always use a good one!) . You may be scouting for funding for a project. You may be after information to help with your Social Media. Either way, the needs are endless, so refine what you want and ensure that's your focus. Also make sure you rehearse your 3 second, 30 second and 3 minute pitch. and remember the 3 seconds needs to be interesting enough to lead into the 30 second and same again into the 3 minute pitch.

2. Do make a good first impression.

For good reason it is said that, you only get that 1 chance for a first impression. A good first impression will keep the individual interested in continuing a conversation and therefore build towards a professional relationship in the future. These are some simple pointers

a) Dress to impress or at least appropriately for the event.
b) Have a firm handshake.
c) Look people in the eye.
d) Smile - it helps people feel comfortable and shows you are friendly and approachable
e) Be attentive.
f) Use leading introductions such as 'Hi Harry, good to meet you. I believe you are a guru in the Marketing space!'
g) Remember and use their name in conversation.
h) Speak clearly
i) Use positive body language – don't slouch, yawn etc

3. Do Listen attentively and with intent.

When you talk to someone, listen attentively to what they are saying so you can better understand their interests, skills, talents and needs. This is vital as you not only want to learn about their background and skills to benefit you, but you also want to understand what their needs are so you can be of benefit them. Instead of just approaching someone and talking for the heck of it, engage the person in interesting and meaningful conversation.

4. Do help others

If no one is helping anyone, what's the point? A great follow on from the above first impressions and a great way to initiate a business networking relationship is to contribute a solution to someone's problem or issue. A simple 'How can I help you? Or 'What challenges are you facing?' will shift the focus off you. People are more comfortable talking about themselves so listen intently and see how you could help with information or with further contacts/introduction. If you consistently position yourself as providing value, you will quickly develop a positive reputation for it and result in people doing the same for you.

5. Do ask for help

This is why you are at the event and people are usually happy to offer support when they can, so don't be nervous and worry about imposing on others. It understandable that people don't want to show they lack knowledge and as a result, they avoid seeking help from others. Remember point 1 above and ensure you ask for the information you need to achieve your objective.

6. Do keep in touch/follow up

This is a major failing and one that, when done correctly, is a differentiator and will have massive positive impact on you and your mission. People are more willing to help when they know what you up to and if your contacts

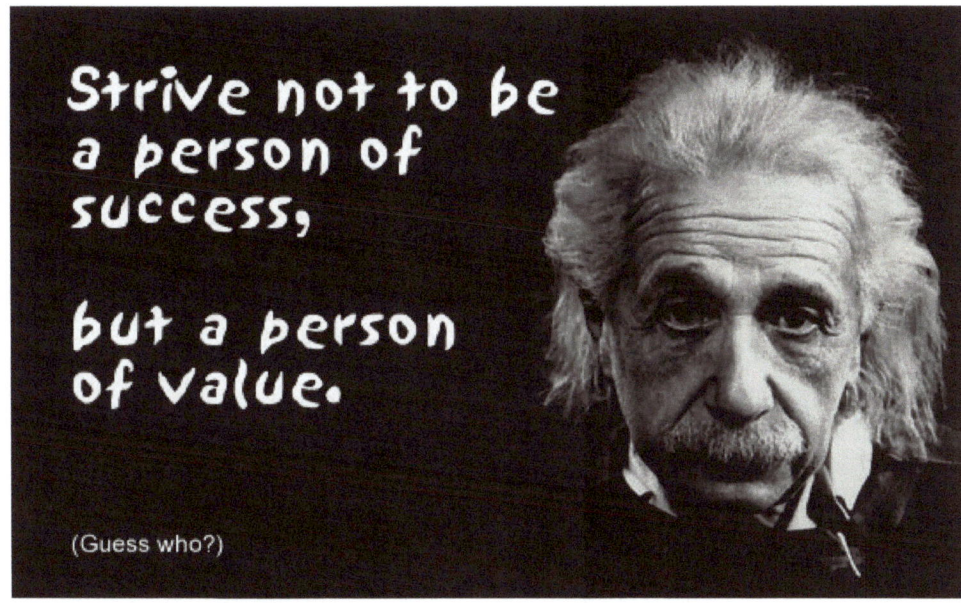

only hear from you when you need something from them, you'll soon find your requests going unanswered. Some tips to improve this are.

a) Follow up the next day to every card you received. Even if you have no intention of doing business, just sending a very brief friendly email or message reminding the person of when and where you met and the positive points from your discussion. This will set you apart from all of those that don't do so – which is most ….

b) Periodically reconnect with contacts and don't allow your relationships to dwindle. Again even if there is no immediate need for business you can forward an interesting article or relevant blog post to keep those connections strong. You can also update people on your current events or ask about what's new in theirs.

7. Do give to get.

Networking shouldn't be a one-way street. Be a person of value and give information freely. Ask what can you do for your network? If you come across an interesting article or a relevant job listing, share it with your network. Content is the new currency, so if you willingly share information that's of benefit to others, it won't be long till they willingly search out and reciprocate whenever they can.

8. Do say thank you

It's strange that this needs to be a point as it's a blatant essential, but I have seen it omitted time and time again. Failing to thank contacts when they provide help can come across as rude, as though you are taking their help for granted and you run the risk of jeopardising your relationships and reputation. A simple "thank you" may sound trivial, but demonstrates your appreciation for them.

Dependant on the situation a simple verbal thank you may be OK, but a thank you note, social media post, call or gift (when appropriate) will always be remembered. You never know when your paths may cross again.

9. Do be a person of integrity and trust.

Integrity should be the at the top of everyone's values and is one of the most important aspects in building a relationship based on trust. You need to create a 'brand' of integrity thought doing what you say, following through and remaining honest in your dealings when networking. This will help your network connections grow to trust you, knowing that you have integrity and their best interests in mind.

10. Do practice networking

The more you practice anything the better you will get, so the more you network, the more you will grow in confidence and improve your prospects

In the next article we will cover the all important 'Don'ts' in the networking environment so please come back so we can all learn and grow together.

HOW TO MANAGE YOUR BUSINESS'S GLOBAL COMPLIANCE RISKS, WITH LESSONS FROM FACEBOOK

BY JOHN BOSTWICK, HEAD OF CONTENT MANAGEMENT, VISTRA (USA)

Facebook's early company motto, "**Move fast and break things**," should appeal to any entrepreneur. It has a clarion ring and implies a disdain for bureaucratic sluggishness and courage in the face of risk.

It should also give pause to any serious businessperson. The phrase encourages recklessness and a naïve disdain for any kind of controls, from developmental to ethical to regulatory. Facebook's founder **Mark Zuckerberg** conceded as much when he changed the famous tagline in 2014 to the less catchy but wiser, "Move fast with stable infra". The revision implied that the risks of heedlessly developing code aren't worth the potential rewards. There are of course countless risks associated with running a business, from the developmental risks highlighted by Zuckerberg to financial, operational, strategic, and more. Zuckerberg's decision to buy Instagram for $1 billion in 2012, for example, struck many at the time as not only risky but positively reckless. The risk paid off, though, and Bloomberg now estimates Instagram is worth a hundred times what Zuckerberg paid for it.

Compliance-related risks are different. They're a cost of doing business rather than a source of potential windfalls. But like other risks, they must be properly managed or they can have profoundly negative effects.

Facebook has lessons for us in this area too. In July of this year, the U.S. Federal Trade Commission announced the tech giant must pay a $5 billion penalty for failing to comply with an FTC order related to user privacy. The fine is the largest ever imposed by the U.S. for any violation.

Immediately following the FTC announcement, many commentators said the financial penalty could easily be absorbed by Facebook, which was reported to have had $40 billion in cash reserves. These commentators were essentially saying Facebook had been slapped on the wrist, which is another way of saying that, all things considered, Zuckerberg had effectively managed his compliance risks.

I think that view is short-sighted. To begin with, the FTC order has consequences beyond the financial. It wrests significant control from Facebook's leadership, requiring the company to establish an independent privacy committee of the board of directors and designate compliance officers to oversee Facebook's privacy program, among other things. The order also caused reputational damage, which is hard to quantify but clearly a concern for Zuckerberg, as it must be for any business leader. During the FTC investigation, Zuckerberg published a 3,200-word blog post reassuring Facebook's users and investors—and, presumably, FTC authorities—that his company was committed to "building a privacy-focused messaging and social networking platform … and … working openly and consulting with experts across society as we develop this." This measured rhetoric about the importance of protecting user privacy—no matter how cynically you take it—is almost certainly a form of reputational damage control and stands in vivid contrast to Zuckerberg's early injunction to "move fast and break things."

Perhaps most importantly, the FTC penalty comes from only one jurisdiction, the U.S. In today's economy, virtually **all significant businesses**—and obviously Facebook—**operate in multiple countries**. Ominously for Facebook, the FTC penalty sets a record-breaking standard for authorities outside the U.S. In an article titled Regulators Around the World Are Circling Facebook, The New York Times reports that Australia, France, Germany, India, Ireland, New

Zealand, Singapore and the UK are separately scrutinizing Facebook's data privacy practices, or they've actually passed or are considering new restrictions on the company.

This highlights one critical fact of running a business in our global economy: **Companies don't just have to follow the rules of their home country**, they have to follow the **rules of all the countries** where they do business. And each country has many—I was about to say countless—regulations, including those related to permanent establishment (i.e. creating a taxable presence), worker classification, immigration, employee benefits, anti-money laundering, data protection, and more.

Few of us can relate to Facebook's historic commercial success. But the company's progression from taking a "move fast and break things" approach to compliance, to incurring penalties, to taking a more considered approach to compliance is a common one.

A growing business should know that there's no need to go through these compliance-related growing pains. You can learn from studying others' mistakes and from their best practices. In other words, you can bypass the stage when a company is either ignorant or dismissive of regulatory obligations, and the stage when it inevitably incurs financial and **reputational damage as a result.** One of the best ways to **protect your organization** is to develop a strong system of internal compliance controls that's appropriate for your business. There are many names for this kind of system or set of processes, such as a centralized international support structure, global operations risk management framework, internal infrastructure, and so on. I'll call it an international support structure here, but you can call it whatever makes sense for you and your business.

I'll pause here to emphasize that I'm not advocating for a bureaucratic model that hampers productivity and exists primarily to perpetuate itself rather than **provide value to the organization**. It should without saying that kind of thing must be avoided at all costs. Your own international support structure should be developed and implemented with an eye towards efficiently and effectively lowering cross-border compliance risks. It should embody the maxim "an ounce of prevention is worth a pound of cure."

1. **The first step in creating an effective** and lasting international support structure is to create a **central team** responsible for overseeing **global activities**. Depending on the size of the company and extent of its international activities, members of the team should include one or more representatives from finance, tax, HR, the general counsel's office, and risk management. In most cases, you'll need to vet and hire a third-party service provider that specializes in international expansion to help you make informed decisions. If you're happy with their advice after working with them, you'll almost certainly want to retain their services to help you vet new activities and monitor existing ones. (If you're not happy with them, by all means hire someone else.) Ideally, you should form your international team before your first expansion so you can properly vet that proposal and establish sound practices for reviewing future proposals. With the help of your third-party provider, the team should consider whether the planned expansion supports the company's mission. It should understand the full budget implications of the expansion, including what it costs and how long it takes to establish a legal entity, hire and terminate local employees, send expat employees, file corporate and indirect taxes, comply with data protection legislation, lease office space, and more. This will of

course be a learning process, but the group will become more knowledgeable and efficient with each new expansion.

2. Once your first international office is established, your **central international team should meet regularly**—once a quarter or whatever is fitting given the number and nature of your activities. At the meetings, the group should vet any new proposals and review existing activities, including cross-border electronic commerce, which can trigger tax and other obligations even if your company doesn't have a physical presence in a country where you have customers. Your third-party expert should keep you apprised of any regulatory changes in the countries where you have activity. The team or a designee should also be in regular contact with a representative of each foreign office to discuss regulatory considerations, company policy changes, and other areas related to maintaining compliant operations.

3. Speaking of policies, your central international team should also be responsible for overseeing the **development of company policies related to international activities**. Many policies will need to account for the unique laws and culture of each country of operation. For example, a locally compliant HR handbook for France-based employees will necessarily be different from an HR handbook for Saudi Arabia-based employees. In short, your policies and procedures will have to be compliant in each country of operation. That said, your company policies should as much as possible be consistent with each other and align with your company values and mission. Some policies—like a tax equalization or tax protection policy for employees you send on assignment—should be consistent across jurisdictions, in part to position yourself as a fair employer and promote employee engagement. You'll also want to consider developing policies related to opening bank accounts abroad, vetting and paying vendors, leasing office space, hiring independent contractors and employees, sending expats, protecting data, and complying with anti-corruption regulations.

4. In addition to establishing regular communication between your central international team and representatives from your foreign offices, you'll need to **establish effective and regular communications with and trainings for all your employees** to ensure they follow policies. It's worth emphasizing that any company initiative that hopes to be successful needs vocal support from leadership. If Mark Zuckerberg can take the time to write a 3,200-word blog post about the importance of protecting user privacy, you or another leader should be able to take the time to write 200- to 500-word emails or make videos stressing the importance of following your organization's global compliance policies.

5. Those policies should be available in a single, easily accessible repository for your employees, such as an intranet. You should also **create a single, secure repository (with limited access) for all documents related to your international operations**. These may include proposals for new international activities, central international team meeting minutes, office lease agreements, partnership agreements, bank accounts and their authorized signers, articles of incorporation for your entities, foreign employment and contractor agreements, financial reports, tax returns and other statutory filings, along with a list of employees working outside their home countries.

6. That last point is a critical and often-overlooked one. Employers should **track all expatriate assignments, even short-term cross-border business trips**. Some larger companies invest heavily to track their employees' cross-border trips and related expenses, sometimes through their HR/ERP platforms, because the risks are considerable. Depending on the length of stay(s), activities performed, any applicable double taxation treaties, and other factors, these cross-border assignments can trigger tax and/or filing obligations, immigration requirements (such as work permits), requirements to disclose physical presence, and more. **Regulations in jurisdictions around the world** are changing rapidly and sometimes radically to account for our **digitalized global economy**, income inequality, mass migration, and other factors. The Organisation for Economic Co-operation and Development's BEPS initiative—which seeks to prevent multinationals from shifting profits to low- or no-tax jurisdictions where they don't actually engage in significant consumer-facing activity—is one prominent example of **how countries are working together to implement new ways** of regulating business activities. Given heightened public awareness and the ability of authorities everywhere to monitor economic activities, it's more important than ever for **multinational businesses** to understand these trends and specific laws.

Unfortunately for **multinational businesses**, there are still no global regulations, only country-specific ones and some regulations that apply to blocs, like the **EU's General Data Protection Regulation.** Keeping track of and **understanding new laws and changes to existing laws in each country** of operation remains one of the most difficult aspects of running a compliant global business. Finding a third party to do this job for you is likely your most cost-effective and least risky means of accomplishing this step. Implementing the kind **of international support structure** described here will help ensure your organization is reasonably equipped to comply with regulations once you do grasp them.

ENGLISH ACCESS GAUTENG

Thierno Abdoul Aziz Diallo, Owner and Managing Director of English Access Gauteng being interviewed by Dean Graham - The #1 Branding and Sales Authority - in South Africa.

BY DEAN GRAHAM (SOUTH AFRICA)

Thierno Abdoul Aziz Diallo, Owner and Managing Director of English Access Gauteng, took over the international language school in January 2018, after relocating to South Africa with his family. He is originally from Mauritania but has also previously lived Germany and Ghana and has gathered extensive international experience from engaging in international Sports and Development. Since 1997, he has been actively supporting Youth Development by founding the Mauritanian Wushu Kung-Fu Federation, representing Mauritania in the Arab and African League and by teaching Wushu Kung-Fu and Self Defense classes. Thierno understands the vital importance of mastering language skills when crossing boundaries.

1. Dean: Thierno as a world citizen yourself, what benefits do you see in studying English Abroad?

I have learnt the importance of the requirement for global communication and cross-cultural understanding first hand from the moment I crossed boarders myself. With the current advancement in communication and technology, the world has opened up and the requirement for English has grown significantly. Studying abroad does not only offer you the ability to learn English in a native speaking country, but also gives you an experience you will never forget. It gives you the opportunity to immerse yourself in another culture and also to experience the power of global cultural exchange. It is truly a life changing experience.

2. Dean: Why did you take on English Access Gauteng?

I view it as a great opportunity and privilege to run this language school and what we do contributes to self development; whether they are foreign nationals joining us for the English Foreign Language (EFL) program, native English speakers taking part in our Teaching English as a Foreign Language (TEFL) program or those taking Zulu or Business English classes. We all grow through languages, whether it is for private or professional reasons. My main reason for taking on English Access Gauteng is being part of making a difference in people's lives.

3. Dean: How would you describe the opportunities of a TEFL teacher after becoming certified to teach English for Foreign Learners?

An English native speaker has so many opportunities by becoming a TEFL certified teacher. Some dream of travelling the world while earning a living through teaching while others want to contribute to the development of underprivileged adults and children here in South Africa. The ultimate mission of English Access Gauteng is to develop confidence in all our students through helping them achieve their personal and professional goals. We do not only have an impact on our students, but the school also contributes through offering free English classes to those who do not have the financial means themselves to pay for the courses. It is a very rewarding experience for our TEFL graduates as they teach and share their knowledge.

4. Dean: What is your Ultimate goal/Vision?

My vision is to offer high quality teaching in a friendly and international environment and that is exactly what English Access Gauteng stands for!

5. Dean: What is your current secret to business success in the education sector, as the current leader of English training/positioning in South Africa?

At English Access Gauteng we have core values and we believe in respect, reliability, commitment, consistency, discipline and the delivery of quality lessons. We stand for what we do and for the products we offer. We constantly strive to improve our programs and courses so that we offer the highest quality of teaching to our students. We are a full member of Education South Africa (EduSA) and being certified by the DHET confirms this. We constantly communicate with our current and former students and closely follow their personal development. Enhancing our students opportunities in life is precious to us and seeing that they do this with joy and dedication whilst being at our school is extremely rewarding. The key to success for me is believing in growing through language in every possible way and in making a difference.

STOCKHOLM:
THE UNICORN FACTORY OF THE WORLD

BY ASA GRANBERG (SWEDEN)

How come the small country of Sweden with a population of only 10 million, of which one million lives in the capital of Stockholm, is considered to rival Silicon Valley as the tech unicorn factory of the world?

Well, some claim that it is the well-developed tech ecosystem in Sweden and in particular in Stockholm that is the foundation in the recent years to tech Unicorns like Spotify, Klarna, Izettle, Mojang (creator of Minecraft), Skype, King and Truecaller just to name a few.

Every week there are many tech events and seminars all around Stockholm and most of them are free events. On top of that, Stockholm offers the "STHLM TECH FEST" week which is a whole week filled with many tech events, evening mingles and seminars regarding different tech related subjects as well as so called "hackathons".

The tech fest week finally ends up in the grand finale, which is a large Tech Conference day where several thousands of tech entrepreneurs, investors, tech specialists and all other categories from the tech ecosystem

gather and listen to seminars and panel discussions and walk around the sponsor booths. All these events are facilitating networking and connecting all tech interested people. This results in new co-working and new innovative co-operations to start ups and everyone can keep up to date and find the competencies and connections they need to evolve whatever tech project they are working on or would like to work on.

But is it really the built-up tech-ecosystem in Stockholm that is the reason for Stockholm being appointed as the second major tech-start-up-hub right after Silicon Valley?

This subject of why Stockholm has managed to become the second major tech-start-up-hub was discussed on one of the panel debates at the STHLM TECH FEST Conference in September 2019. Well, the panel concluded that it partly is due to the well evolved tech-ecosystem that Stockholm has become such a strong Start-Up hub in the world. Additionally, it might be because the politicians in Sweden on all levels have understood the impact of the Swedish tech-ecosystem, making the politicians provide a lot of resources e.g.; start-up or event spaces, funds and various public sector start-up consultancy agencies.

However, the panel added to the analysis that for once the so-called Swedish culture of "the law of Jante" or in Swedish "Jantelagen" could be a key factor to the tech innovations development speed. The "jantelagen" is the unofficial subculture of Swedish people being fostered into understanding that nobody is better than anyone else and all humans have equal rights and equal value.

The reason for "jantelagen" nourishing innovations, according to the tech-fest panel, is that it makes organisations in Sweden extremely flat and not hierarchic. This, since everyone is considered to having the same values, implies that a junior team member can go straight to a very senior team member or even the corporate management and ask for assistance or ask questions or explain an issue.

This allows for information to travel swiftly and problems and issues get addressed and solved immediately instead of having to travel a hierarchic journey up by the "correct" managers in one part of a corporate "silo" and then down to the destination in the other corporate "silo", like it happens within a traditional corporate culture.

In Sweden, it is common to go straight to the destination instead of waiting in line. So, information travels horizontal and not vertical, making it a very quick production- and problem-solving process.

One more typical Swedish subcultural feature

is the "consensus" seeking process that is built into the Swedish society. This feature was brought up by the Tech Fest panel as a motivational factor, meaning that if everyone has agreed to a decision then people are motivated instead of hesitant to executing something that they otherwise could be opponent to.

The "consensus" seeking culture and the "jantelagen" would then be Sweden's biggest assets and a good ground for co-operations. And according to the panel, it is really good cooperation that breeds innovations from ideas to Unicorns.

Maybe, the panel above made a correct analysis of the situation and maybe there are many other components to Sweden and Stockholm being considered as the start-up capital of Europe and the 'unicorn factory' of the world.

However, one thing is certain: The Swedish Start Up and Tech environment is currently boiling hot and the Swedish Unicorns are hitting the world and the stock exchanges like never before. If you are looking to invest in technology and innovation, then you will want to turn your eyes to the Swedish market!

Asa Granberg

Aimhill Consulting Group

www.aimhill.com

70 YEARS OF FRIENDSHIP BETWEEN GERMANY AND THE USA

BY SUE BAUMGÄRTNER-BARTSCH (GERMANY)

When you get invited for a royal event at the Residence in Munich Germany, you know life has a bigger purpose in store. It was an honor to be part of such an elegant event where tea was served in Silver tea pots, and guests from government, industry and society were invited to gather in one place. This year, we are looking back at 70 years of history and celebrated the 70th Silver tea on November 6 2019.

In 1949, this charity event was brought to life through the actions of Sam E. Woods, the then US-Consul General in Munich, who invited guests to his home in order to collect donations for the suffering people of Munich, Germany. Fifty guests accepted his invitation and the event was so successful that the women of the German-American Women's Club of Munich decided to repeat the Silver Tea every year.

Bavarian State Minister Dr. Florian Herrmann emphasized in his speech that the pursuit of happiness is nowadays more important than ever. He stated that our success as a country is connected with that of the Americans.

Traudl Schmid, as the president of the German American Women's Club ("GAWC") made everyone in the audience aware that there was this one sentences that stood the test of time, and that was so crucial in developing the relationship between Germans and Americans. A sentence that is so simple yet so important: "How can we help"? is what the Americans said to the Germans in 1949 to help the people of Munich rebuild.

What made the evening so special was also the visit from Meghan Gregonis, U.S. Consul General in Munich, as she was about to travel further to visit Berlin that month to be part of the 30 years of reunification of Germany.

What was once divided has been united. And friendship among human beings is what makes the difference. Meghan in her speech about the reunification emphasized that aspect of human friendship and opportunities between Germans and Americans. It was beautiful to see so many people being witness to this event.

Chairlady Susanne Ahrens has been responsible for the overall organization of the Silver Tea and opened up the buffet. The historic ambience sparkled with silver platters of beautifully arranged canapes and the highest quality tea was served from silver tea pots. Receipts form this charity event allow to support the German-American Student Exchange program amongst others.

As I like to say: "Students are the future entrepreneurs!" Let's inspire them and let us empower them. One of the exchange students was present at the event to share his experience and thanking for this opportunity to learn beyond what one can see in one country, but to meet other people, other nations, and to learn from each other.

The evening gave opportunity to meet Germans, Americans and people from various walks of life-all with the notion of helping each other. It was wonderful to see people connecting, ideas exchanged, and new business opportunities ignited.

Be courageous, be open-minded and ask how you can help, and you will see what doors will open.

USING GEO-FENCING IN ONLINE ADVERTISING
"THE BEST WAY TO TARGET PEOPLE WHO ALREADY ARE WANTING TO BUY!"

BY ANDREW WALKER (UNITED KINGDOM)

When companies push out advertising into the market they reach an audience that is not going to buy, one that is considering to buy and one that extremely wanting to buy such products or services.

Entrepreneurs and marketing agencies usually set in a ads campaign a region or a range around the company's premises to show ads to the internet users. If you are a local car dealer then you need to have a very special niche (e.g. bullet proof vehicles) in the market to justify to advertise on a national scale. Most car dealerships should focus on a region of 40-120 miles around their show room. This is due to the fact that most dealerships are connected with one of the few main automotive brands (e.g. Ford, Toyota, BMW).

When you look at what might help you increase the return of investment on your online ads, you need to recognize that sometimes targeting a region might bring along a far too high rate of non-buyers. These are people who see your ads but either can not afford or do not need a car. You need to find those can afford and might buy one as their car broke down or they would desire an upgrade. If someone has decided to buy now a new car they are actively looking at brands, models and options. They are often overwhelmed by the range of opportunities and need a smart sales person to guide them towards the right product.

So that is where geofencing or geo-targeting allows us to target city districts and even better preferred buildings. Let us say you are a estate agent and need to fill your funnel with people want to buy a new house?

Then the best is to go to do a geo fence around locations such as other property agents, banks and popular areas people go to find properties on offer.

Why is this so special for targeting niche leads? Well, each time a social media user enters that location (real estate office) we will show the potential buyer our ads. When he leaves the area, we will continue to retarget him over the next few days. So, we can show him or her a variety of ads. The opportunity is massive but if you do it the wrong way you will not get them to engage with your business.

We need to have specially arranged images and text for these ads. You can not expect the person to see your ad and run into your office to become your client. We need to nurture the audience with relevant content and in the right way that matches the culture of the platform where we place that content.

Do not be the bull in the porcelain shop that breaks all the china. Have the right situational awareness. Platforms like Facebook and Instagram do not like you to violate their ads policies. Being greedy or disrespectful with your banners and content can get your ads account disables or even restricted. Yes, such a situation is horrible but even when you play by the rules your account and ads can be disapproved. Nevertheless, there are ways to reduce the risk and handle situations where Facebooks artificial intelligence decides to disable or block your advertising accounts.

Let us say, you have a care product for horses. How do I go about promoting this? Well, who will buy that product? Is it the horse owner, the stable that is renting out the stable box to the horse owner, or is it a medical professional or an authority? So, we have now several people in mind that could potentially buy our product.

Next is to go and ask people who have horses. They know who buys the stuff. Then ask that person and get as much filed information. Now we have a better idea who might be the buyer (stable owner or horse owner) and the influencer (e.g. other horse owners or the doctor).

Where would I have to go to meet these people outside of the stables? Do I have to go to a café or to pet shops or an exhibition for horses or a horse racing area to find these people?

Let's say we want to target everyone at a specialized shop for horse equipment. Well there we will definitely not run into people who have a dog but no horse. Let's put a geo-fence around that shop.

Now our ads platform knows we want to get in touch with everyone who goes there. This way our ads will be super targeted at people who are most likely horse owners or take care of horses. We will always have people who have no horse but are interested in the equipment but not in our product.

Nevertheless, this geofencing massively increases the efficiency of our ads campaign that eventually will drive leads into our funnel that leads them directly into becoming buyers.

Depending on the platform we can reduce the targeted area to an area size of 150 feet or 45 meters. You could target one particular shop in a big shopping complex with the right geo data.

Do that in your target region 30 or 80 times and you are placing your ads right in front of people who are highly potential future buyers. This leads to a better return of investment for your ads budget. www.prmediareach.com

www.ingramcontent.com/pod-product-compliance
Lightning Source LLC
Chambersburg PA
CBHW051826210526
45473CB00005B/1762